WE CAN DO HARD THINGS

One Boy's Journey to Finding Courage and Confidence Within

By Colton and Ryan Sawyer

Illustrated By Aurora Guertin

Copyright © 2024 IHP Coaching

All rights reserved.

No part of this publication may be reproduced, distributed, or transmitted in any form or by any means, including photocopying, recording, or other electronic or mechanical methods, without the prior written permission of the publisher or author.

www.ihpcoaching.com

Written by Colton Sawyer & Ryan Sawyer

Book Cover by Aurora Guertin

Illustrations by Aurora Guertin

ISBN 978-1-7354824-3-9

Foreword: Embracing Strength Amid Life's Challenges

In a world where the journey from childhood to adulthood can be strewn with hurdles like self-doubt, bullying, lack of focus, and the challenges of conditions like ADD/ADHD, Colton's book, "WE CAN DO HARD THINGS," serves as a guiding light for those who may find themselves navigating these difficult terrains. It's a powerful testament to the strength found in embracing our uniqueness, especially during moments of adversity.

Many of us have, at some point, felt the weight of self-doubt or struggled to fit in during their formative years (and often well into adulthood). We may now be facing one of the issues mentioned, so Colton's story is a reminder that even when confronted with these formidable challenges, there's a well of strength within us waiting to be discovered.

Colton's journey began with the transformative experience of SEALFIT's "Unbeatable Mind" training alongside his father. It was this shared experience of doing hard things, as a team and with a swim buddy (in his case, his Dad), that became a catalyst for Colton's transformation. He realized that such an experience could be the medicine that many others need, serving as a path to resilience and empowerment.

As you turn the pages of "WE CAN DO HARD THINGS," I encourage you to embark on this journey with an open heart and an open mind. Colton's message is simple yet profound: you have the capacity to build your confidence, face adversity head-on, and rise above the challenges that may come your way.

This book is an invitation to embrace your uniqueness and confront life's difficulties with courage and resilience. It's a rallying cry for teenagers who may be grappling with self-confidence issues, bullying, focus challenges, or the allure of drugs. Colton's message is a testament to the extraordinary strength within each of you, waiting to be harnessed and celebrated.

So, as you delve into Colton's words in "WE CAN DO HARD THINGS," remember that his journey is not just his own; it's a beacon of hope and inspiration for all who may face similar challenges. The world is eager to witness your unique brilliance and strength. Are you ready to embrace the transformative power of doing hard things together, just as Colton did with his father at SEALFIT?

You can do hard things, and in doing so, unlock your true potential and become the best version of yourself. The strength you seek is already within you, waiting to be unleashed.

You've got this, easy day... Hooyah!

Mark Divine

Founder, SEALFIT

NYT Best Selling Author The Way of the SEAL, Unbeatable Mind, 8 Weeks to SEALFIT

Contents

Foreword: Embracing Strength Amid Life's Challenges   iii

Introduction   1

Chapter 1: Pushed to the Edge   2

Chapter 2: Where It All Started   4

Chapter 3: Making the Commitment   8

Chapter 4: Finding My WHY   10

Chapter 5: Choosing Courage   13

Chapter 6: Going All-In   16

Chapter 7: How I Got My Nickname   18

Chapter 8: Facing Fear   20

Chapter 9: Ice Bath   22

Chapter 10: It's All About the Team   24

Chapter 11: Lessons Learned   26

Chapter 12: What's Now Possible   29

Final Thoughts   30

Reader Questions   31

Introduction

Are you someone who sometimes feels alone, struggles to fit in, gets picked on or even bullied at times?

I can relate. My name is Colton, I'm eleven years old now but at the time of this story I was nine. When I first started elementary school, I didn't feel like I fit in with the other kids. I was bullied over the years, called names, made fun of on a regular basis, and one time I was even punched in the face. I didn't know how to stand up for myself when other kids were picking on me. I really let it bother me and it made me doubt myself. This made it hard to be happy and excited about life. I lacked the confidence to be true to myself and let my unique gifts and talents shine.

My goal for you is that you learn how to build your confidence and give yourself permission to be unique, to be different and to not follow the crowd.

The world needs all of us to be our strongest selves because we are the leaders of tomorrow. I believe that everything we experience in life can make us stronger.

Think about that while you read this book.

Chapter 1:
Pushed to the Edge

I am freezing cold, lying in our hotel room bed with blankets wrapped around me. My dad is on the phone with coach Rob to make sure that he is doing all the right things to help me recover. A few minutes later, there's a knock on the door. It's coach Rob. He walks over to the edge of the bed where I'm lying and says, "Hey Stingray. How are you doing, buddy?"

I replied, "I think I am doing better," even though I was still feeling tired and weak.

A moment later Coach Rob said, "Don't worry. This is a good thing. You just pushed yourself to your edge and got stronger because of it." His saying that made me feel much better and it made me feel a bit stronger too. As Coach Rob walked out of the room, he looked back and said, "I'll see you guys at lunch in a few minutes."

Less than five minutes later I threw the blankets off me and jumped out of bed shouting, "Let's get back to the team. I feel fine!" We headed back down to the training to reunite with the team. When I came back to the conference room where the other teammates were eating lunch, everybody seemed excited to see me back and I was happy to be back with them. I felt so supported after going through this weekend with the Unbeatable Mind team, I felt like I had an army behind me in life, which made me realize something I'd never understood before– Anything is possible when you are a part of a team.

I had faced some of my biggest fears and gotten stronger. I'll share more about that later.

Chapter 2:
Where It All Started

You might be wondering why a nine-year-old boy was inspired to train with former Navy Seals. I'll tell you how it all started, but first, I need to take you back a few years. It all started with my dad leaving on trips. I always hated it when he left, but I knew that he was doing it to be the best version of himself. After watching him leave to learn how to train his mind, it made me curious, and I started to wonder if I could learn how to make myself better like my dad did. After one of his trips, I told my dad, "The next time you go to train with the UM (Unbeatable Mind) team, I want to come," my dad kind of laughed and said, "Maybe someday Bud, but you are too young."

Looking back, I think my dad was right. I really wasn't ready for this yet. At the time, I was feeling frustrated at school. When I went out to recess it seemed like everyone was in groups playing games, laughing and having a good time, and I was stuck on the outside. I felt so left out that I wanted to do anything to fit in and be cool. This led me to make a bad choice when I came back from recess. Let's just say I did something inappropriate to try and make people laugh. This choice and others I had made around that time got me in trouble with my dad. My dad was very disappointed and taught me about what he calls the Trust Bank.

The Trust Bank is how much someone can trust you because of the decisions that you make every day. Since I got in such big trouble, the Trust Bank got completely drained. My dad taught me the difference between rights and privileges. Each human being has rights: the right to food, shelter, education and safety.

He taught me that everything else is a privilege, like playing sports, watching tv, hanging out with friends, playing video games and having treats.

He used this opportunity to teach me by taking away all my privileges and told me that I could earn them back as I refilled the Trust Bank.

Of everything he said, one thing stood out to me the most. He told me that if you don't learn how to train your mind you will get random results in life, and you'll end up feeling sad and frustrated. But if you use this lesson as a motivator and learn how to be in control of your mind, you will be able to create the life that you want and learn that life can be fun and exciting.

As I began to earn back my dad's trust, I asked him if I could train with him every day, so I could go to the Unbeatable Mind Experience and learn to train my mind. He welcomed me but warned me that he was not going to hold my hand, and it wasn't going to be easy. I would have to set my own alarm and be ready to train in our garage gym at 5:30am. "Okay I'm in," I told him. We began to do some workouts and training together in the mornings.

The next time my dad was getting ready to leave on another Unbeatable Mind training trip, I told him to ask Mark Divine (leader of the Unbeatable Mind team) if I could go to the next Unbeatable Mind Experience.

When my dad returned, he told me that Mark said, "YES as long as you are READY!" This is totally awesome, I thought to myself.

Then I asked my dad, "What do I need to do to be ready?"

Chapter 3:
Making the Commitment

"Let's first discuss what to expect, so you know what you are saying yes to," said my dad. He continued to tell me that this event isn't really designed for kids, and that the youngest to experience it in the past was a 16-year-old. He continued that it was an event that involved different areas of personal development. There were going to be mental, emotional and physical challenges. As I listened to him tell me about the challenges that I would have to overcome. It made me a bit nervous, and I wondered if I was going to be able to do it.

My dad then taught me the first rule to winning in life is to see the end before you begin. So, we practiced by closing our eyes and picturing ourselves at the end of the weekend being proud of how we showed up and who we became in the process.

He then taught me the second rule to winning in life, which is to train your mind and body to be prepared for challenges.

He quoted a Navy Seal by saying in life:
"You do not rise to occasion; you fall to your level of training."

He then said, "To make sure you are ready for the event, so you are able to learn what you need to learn from this opportunity, you must commit to training your mind and body." This gave me three months to train and prepare. My training included a cold shower every morning, 10 minutes of breath and mindfulness practice, daily physical training, and a weekly ice bath. I committed without much hesitation, but I didn't fully understand how hard this would be.

Chapter 4:
Finding My WHY

The first two weeks of the training were a bit rough. Let's just say that I didn't exactly crush it in the beginning. I hit snooze and fell back to sleep a couple of times, I forgot to do my breath and mindfulness practice, and I skipped the cold shower a few times.

I struggled to stay consistent and really started to question why I wanted to go to the Unbeatable Mind Experience. My Dad was being somewhat patient, but I wasn't sure why. I now know that he was letting me fall, so I could learn how to get back up and be more focused.

In those two weeks, every time I missed part of my training, Dad would find a way to make it harder. After one of our makeup sessions for what I'd missed my dad asked me, "Why do you think you are struggling to be consistent with your training plan?" I replied," I notice that I get confused and think, "Why am I trying to do this?" My dad said, "PERFECT!" with his loud coaching voice. "Let's do a practice called the 5 Whys to figure that out."

My Dad asked me, "Why are you doing this?"

Why #1: "Because I want to be STRONG." Dad asked, "Ok, why do you want to get stronger?"

Why #2: "Because I want to be able to stand up for myself," Dad asked, "Why do you want to be able to stand up for yourself?"

Why #3: "So I can be who I want to be." Dad asked, "Why do you want to be who you want to be?"

Why #4: "I want to know I can do hard things." Dad then asked one more question, "Why do you want to know you can do hard things?"

Why #5: "I want to show myself and others what is possible when you believe in yourself!"

After I answered that final question, my dad said, "Now that is a reason that will get you out of bed in the morning!"

I felt a new inspiration and motivation that I had never felt before. When I thought about the difference this experience could make for other kids like me, I didn't have a choice. I had to keep going!

Why #1: Because I want to be STRONG.

Why #2: Because I want to stand up for myself.

Why #3: So I can be who I want to be.

Why #4: I want to know I can do hard things.

Why #5: I want to show myself and others what's possible when you believe in yourself!

Chapter 5:
Choosing Courage

Do you know that there are two voices in your head? One voice makes you stronger, more resilient and unlimited. The other voice is making you weaker, more scared, and is limiting you. These two voices can be called the limited mind and unlimited mind or maybe you have heard of them as the **Fear Wolf** and **Courage Wolf** from Tale of the Two Wolves.

The Tale of Two Wolves

> *An old Cherokee is teaching his grandson about life. "A fight is going on inside me," he said to the boy. "It is a terrible fight, and it is between two wolves. One is evil – he is anger, envy, sorrow, regret, greed, arrogance, self-pity, guilt, resentment, inferiority, lies, false pride, superiority, and ego."*
>
> He continued, *"The other is good – he is joy, peace, love, hope, serenity, humility, kindness, benevolence, empathy, generosity, truth, compassion, and faith. The same fight is going on inside you – and inside every other person, too."*
>
> The grandson thought about it for a minute and then asked his grandfather, *"Which wolf will win?"*
>
> The old Cherokee simply replied, *"The one you feed."*
>
> - Unknown

I had heard of this story but did not fully understand what it meant until it was time for my first ice bath. If you have never done an ice bath where you dunk your head under freezing cold ice water for 10 seconds, this is when the Fear Wolf shows up the most!

Important Note: *Never try cold exposure alone. You should always have an adult with you to make sure you are doing it safely and in case of emergency.*

The first time we loaded up the tub with water and ice to practice we started with only a couple bags of ice. It was still cold enough to get all my attention. As I began to get into the tub, I heard a voice in my head that said, "I don't want to do this, this is crazy, what if this kills me?" The fear almost stopped me, but then I remembered the Tale of Two Wolves, and since I knew it was just the Fear Wolf, I told myself, "I can do hard things." I then closed my eyes and saw myself at the end out of the tub with my arms in the air and felt what it would feel like to accomplish this ice bath.

My dad then asked me, "Why are you doing this?" I remembered my WHY and responded, "To show myself and others what is possible."

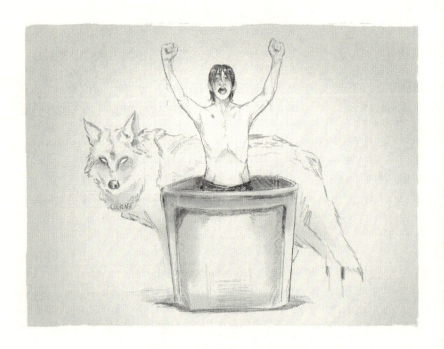

I asked my dad to count down for me. He smiled and said, "5-4-3-2-1," and I dunked my head. I stayed in the water for as long as I could. When I came up, I jumped out of the tub and threw my arms in the air, and it felt exactly like what I saw in my mind before I began.

Chapter 6:
Going All-In

What my dad didn't tell me until later was that I didn't make it the full 10 seconds on my first couple of ice baths. He let me think that I had made it to help me build my confidence. Every week we added another bag of ice to the tub to make the water colder.

Every week it got harder to overcome the Fear Wolf. The more ice that was in the tub, the louder the voice got. This time we filled up the tub with four large bags of ice. Then we checked the temperature, and it was 40 degrees. I stepped into the tub to test the water, and the Fear Wolf kicked in stronger than ever before. I got right back out of the tub and didn't want to do it. This is when my dad and I created what we call BADA. (Breath, Attention, Decide, Act)

My dad said to me, "When life gets hard, we have two choices. To give in or to go all-in."

He asked me what I wanted to do. I said, "I want to go all-in!"

Then he continued by coaching me to control my **BREATH**. He then encouraged me to bring my **ATTENTION** to what's going on inside me (what wolf am I feeding?). Then he asked me to **DECIDE** who I was and who I wanted to be.

Then he told me once you are connected to your breath, and you're aware of what's going on inside you, decide who you want to be and **ACT**.

BADA: Breath, Attention, Decide and Act!

He raised his voice in a powerful and inspiring way and said, "BADA!" I then joined in and said back to him, "BADA! BADA!" I felt this newfound strength and courage, and I dunked my entire body and head. This time I made it the entire 10 seconds!

It worked! I calmed my breathing, noticed what was going on inside me (Fear Wolf), shifted my focus to what was right in front of me, decided who I wanted to be (Courageous), and acted!

That was the birth of BADA and the moment I learned that when life gets hard, go all-in! I took this "all-in" mindset into other areas of my life including school, homework, and chores. Through practicing this mindset, I learned that when you do hard things and go all-in, life gets easier!

Chapter 7:
How I Got My Nickname

We got to California a day early to prepare for the Unbeatable Mind Experience. I had a big fear of the ocean, and I wanted to overcome it. So, we went down to the ocean to feel the water. We started by just putting our feet in. Then, we went in a little bit deeper, until we were up to our waists, and we were playing in the surf.

I was getting comfortable with the ocean and even starting to have some fun. My dad asked, "Are you ready to head back?" I replied, "Yes. I feel confident in the ocean now."

The moment we started to walk back, I felt a sharp sting in my foot, like someone had stabbed me with a knife. I yelled to my dad, "Ahh, my foot!" He looked back with a grin on his face and said, "Stop messing with me!" He thought I was joking around and pretending to get hurt. I yelled, "I'm not kidding, my foot hurts." My dad grabbed me and pulled my foot out of the water and there was a lot of blood, so he picked me up and carried me back to the hotel.

When we got back, my dad grabbed a bucket of ice, thinking that would help. One of our friends walked into the room and immediately knew that I must have been stung by a stingray. He told us to put it in hot water and try to get the venom out. My dad massaged my foot and when the venom came out it was sort of white and gooey looking. After an hour or two I began to feel better. When we told all the UM team the story, the coaches gave me the nickname "STINGRAY."

Chapter 8:
Facing Fear

My fear of the ocean was already strong, then I got hit by a stingray! To make it worse the next day a seal washed up on shore with a big, nasty-looking shark bite out of it. Let's just say this didn't help.

On day two of the event, we loaded the bus early in the morning before sunrise to head to the beach for the famous beach workout the Navy Seals call Beach Games. Beach Games are a nice way of saying they find every way possible to challenge you physically and mentally. They make you dive into the surf then run back to the beach and roll around in the sand until your entire face and body is covered in it. They call that the "sugar cookie." They make you do this over and over. You carry sandbags over your head, do pushups, carry logs, do burpees and everything is done as a team. If one person fails, you must "Hit the surf" which means we ALL go back into the water and get wet and sandy again.

We were standing on the beach as the sun was coming up. Then Coach Rob yelled, "Hit the surf." I felt all the fear and excitement rushing through my body. I took a breath, focused my attention inside, decided to go all-in and let it rip! I took off running towards the water and dove into the surf. I was running so hard that my dad couldn't keep up. My dad and I got in trouble because we were supposed to stay together. We were a swim buddy team which meant we had to stary together no matter what. This was the start of a long, fun and hard morning of physical training. After the Beach Games ended, I felt very happy and proud that I faced my fears and conquered them.

Chapter 9:
Ice Bath

On the final day of the event, my dad reminded me of the first two rules to winning at life.

First: Win in your mind and see the end before you begin.

Second: Train your body and mind to prepare for challenges.

Then he told me the final rule…

Third: When the challenge day arrives- Act and let it rip!

This final rule for success in life was just as important as the first two, my time had come to put it into practice. I was ready to *LET IT RIP!*

We started with our morning physical training as a team while a few of the coaches were preparing the ice baths. Once the ice baths were filled with ice and freezing cold water, the coaches started to call people over two at a time. I watched as these men and women my dad's age overcame the cold of taking the plunge. Every time they called someone over, I felt more and more nervous and excited at the same time. Then it was our turn. "Oh my gosh, holy cow, this is actually happening", I thought to myself. Then I took a deep breath and I thought, "BADA, BADA" and I said, "I've got this!" "I can do hard things."

Dad stepped into the tub first and I got in right after him. The team and coaches started cheering me on. Dad yelled out "BADA, BADA, 3,2,1" and I didn't hesitate, I dunked my head and was not coming up until I knew for sure that I had done the full 10 seconds holding my breath under the freezing water.

It turns out I went over the time and my dad pulled me out of the water. I felt so amazing, I knew for sure that I could do hard things.

This experience taught me that if you prepare hard enough for something, no matter how much it scares you, when the time comes you will be able to fall back on your training and be able to achieve greatness.

Chapter 10:
It's All About the Team

Right after I finished the ice bath, my head hurt, and I started to feel really tired. I was cold and exhausted from the entire weekend.

We jumped right back into training with the team, but it didn't take long for my dad to notice that I wasn't feeling well. He tried to pull me out of the workout and told me that we should go back to the hotel room to get warmed up and rest. There were only a few minutes left in the training. Even though I was exhausted and shivering I said, "No, I am not leaving my team." I would not leave until the team was done training!

My team had supported me as I faced my challenge, and I wasn't about to leave them while they were going through their ice baths no matter how cold or tired, I was. I stayed to support them and got to see each team member finish the ice bath.

Immediately after the team finished, I let my dad take me up to the room to get me warmed up and rest. After I got warmed up and reunited with the team, I remember how excited everyone was to see me feeling better.

Not only did this training strengthen me and teach me so many valuable lessons, but it also helped me understand the power of a TEAM.

Chapter 11:
Lessons Learned

Know Your WHY

When you know WHY you are doing something you can overcome any fear or obstacle. I knew that my WHY was to show myself and others what is possible when you believe in yourself. That made me feel motivated and gave me something to think of when training got hard, or I felt scared.

See the End Before You Begin

There is power in knowing what you want and who you want to be. Seeing where you want to end up makes each step you need to do along the way clearer. Something else I learned is that having a goal in mind can keep you from making bad choices that you will regret.

Train Your Body and Mind

The only way to get better at doing hard things is to do hard things. I practiced doing hard things like training and taking ice baths before the big challenge. Every time I trained, especially on the days I didn't feel like it, it helped me to get better at listening to the Courage Wolf instead of the Fear Wolf.

Place Your Eyes on Others/ TEAM

At the end of the day, the most important thing is the team. Focus on making yourself better, not to be the best, but so you can be a better teammate. Now I think of my family as my home team! We train together to be stronger as a family so we can do hard things and show others what is possible.

Be Careful Listening to The Voice in Your Head

You do not have to listen to any voice in your head that limits you (the Fear Wolf) and instead you can choose to listen to the voice that encourages you (the Courage Wolf). I have even learned that what I watch on TV, the games I play and who I hang out with can make me think differently, so I make sure it's positive and helps me reach my goals.

Go All-In and Face Your Fears

Facing fears makes you stronger. When I faced my fears of going in the ocean and doing the ice bath, I learned that I was capable of so much more than I thought. I also learned that even when something bad happens, like getting stung by a stingray, I can get through it and be okay afterward.

Three Rules for Success in Life

First: Win in your mind and see the end before you begin.

Second: Train your body and mind to prepare for challenges.

Third: When the challenge day arrives, Act and let it rip!

Use BADA

One of the most powerful tools my dad and I created during our time training together was BADA. Saying BADA in my head when I'm training or doing hard things keeps me focused and feeding the Courage Wolf instead of the Fear Wolf.

BADA: Breath, Attention, Decide and Act!

Chapter 12:
What's Now Possible

After this experience, I know I can do hard things. Because of this, I am more confident. Even though some of the bullying has continued, I am able to handle it a lot better than before. I know I am unique, and I want to explore developing my talents and gifts that make me different instead of feeling like I need to fit in.

I am not afraid to try new things like different sports, skateboarding, riding horses, being an author, artist, playing the guitar etc. The funny thing is, the more I focus on being me, the more I'm able to have fun and make new friends!

I know the same thing can be true for you.

I want you to know that you can do hard things, too. We can all be warriors in our own way. You can explore and develop your own unique gifts and talents and maybe you'll be surprised at what you find out about yourself along the way.

Final Thoughts

- Stay open to trying and learning new things, this is how we grow.
- Only compete against yourself, comparison kills joy.
- This journey we are on together called life comes down to two things. First, building trust in yourself which takes discipline. Second is to make the lives of those around you better.
- Embrace and be your best for the teams you are on, including family (that's your home team), sports teams, and at school.
- It's okay to ask for help! I had the idea to write this book to inspire other kids like me. I went to my dad and asked for help. Together we made it happen!

We are all <u>one team</u>, and we can do hard things together.

BADA! BADA!

Reader Questions

1. The only way to get better at doing hard things is to…
2. How does focusing on making yourself better help your team?
3. There are two voices in your head, one that makes you weaker and one that makes you stronger. They are called the ____ wolf and the ____ wolf.
4. In the story, what was the very first fear Colton had to face when he got to California?
5. What was the nickname the team gave Colton?
6. How does "Winning in your mind" or seeing the end before you begin help you reach your goals?
7. Why is it important to know WHY you are trying to reach a goal?
8. Facing your fears makes you _____.
9. What does BADA stand for?
10. What is something new you will try?

Made in United States
Troutdale, OR
03/14/2024

18474744R00022